HAPPINESS IS A DRAG.
Excitement is running high! We're down to the finals.
The race is staged. Tension mounts... and they're off. Look at those super-styled vans jump off the line and streak down the track!
It's close— too close to call.
They're still battling for the lead as the sleek vans flash across the finish line, chutes popping open in a flurry of color and excitement!
And the winner is Drag Vans, from Ohio Art's World of Toys!
OHIO ART
©The Ohio Art Company 1976
DRAG VANS

An AMF Roadmaster bicycle brings out the best in you. The lightest wheels in the world won't win the Tour de France, if you haven't the legs or the stamina.
But the Pacemaker 10-speed makes you look like a pro whether you want to make tracks or merely stay in condition. The tip-off is the name—Roadmaster. Built with

the European touch for balance. And smooth, effortless motion.
And the kicky-looking toys like the Sling and the 3-wheeled Hot Seat stretch younger legs with fun that's made to last.
They're all AMF leisure time products. Made with a reverence for quality and value. The same goes for AMF's Slickcraft power

boats, Voit balls or diving gear, Head skis, or Ben Hogan golf clubs.
So what if you don't qualify for the Six-Day Bike Races!
A Roadmaster bicycle could do wonders for your figure, and that's bringing out the best in you.
AMF Incorporated,
White Plains,
New York 10604.

AMF

AMF brings out the best in you.

Advertisements for Women

Advertisements for Women

Advertisements for Women

Advertisement for Men

Attention male chauvinist pigs.

Relax. When the "Libs" call us names like that it really means they think we're rugged, masculine, virile.
Like these new Hush Puppies. Great styling. Great color.
Plus comfort that just won't quit. Try a pair. From $16. Call us about where to find them. Free.
Dial 800-243-6000   (In Conn., 1-800-942-0655)

They're more than shoes. They're   Hush Puppies

Products of
WOLVERINE
WORLD WIDE   ©1971 Wolverine World Wide, Inc., Rockford, Michigan 49341—makers of Hush Puppies® shoes and boots.

Best Cars Of The 70s

71 Buick GS Sport Coupe

Best Cars Of The 70s

Dodge Challenger R/T

Best Cars Of The 70s

Plymouth Barracuda 'Cuda Hardtop

Best Cars Of The 70s

1977 Pontiac Firebird Trans Am

Top Actors

Marlon Brando

Top Actors

Robert Redford

Top Actors

Jack Nicholson

Top Actresses

Farrah Fawcett

Top Actresses

Diane Keaton

Top Actresses

Faye Dunaway

Famous Icons

Jimmy Carter

Famous Icons

Cesar Chavez

Watergate Scandal

Watergate

Watergate Scandal

Famed Journalist Robert (Bob) Woodward

'Jaws' Movie

First Block Buster Movie

Kitchen Styles

Kitchen Styles

Kitchen Styles

Women's Fashion

Women's Fashion

Women's Fashion

Men's Fashion

Men's Fashion

Men's Fashion

Living Room Décor

'72 Living Room

Living Room Décor

Living Room Décor

Families

Families

Families

Christmas in The 70s

Christmas in The 70s

Christmas 1977

Christmas in The 70s

Acknowledgement
Page No. I Author/s I Title I Source I License